Letters from Home

Our Father's Message of Love

Neil Goodman

MONARCH
BOOKS

Oxford, UK & Grand Rapids, Michigan, USA

First published in the UK in 2007 by
Monarch Books (a publishing imprint of
Lion Hudson plc), Mayfield House,
256 Banbury Road, Oxford OX2 7DH.
Tel: +44 (0)1865 302750
Fax: +44 (0)1865 302757
Email: monarch@lionhudson.com
www.lionhudson.com

ISBN: 978-1-85424-803-9 (UK)
ISBN: 978-0-8254-6155-2 (USA)

Distributed by:
UK: Marston Book Services Ltd, PO Box 269,
Abingdon, Oxon OX14 4YN;
USA: Kregel Publications, PO Box 2607,
Grand Rapids, Michigan 49501

Unless otherwise stated, Scripture quotations are
taken from the Holy Bible, New International
Version, © 1973, 1978, 1984 by the International
Bible Society. Used by permission of
Hodder & Stoughton Ltd. All rights reserved.

British Library Cataloguing Data
A catalogue record for this book is available from
the British Library.

Printed and bound in Malta by Gutenberg Press.

About the Author

Neil Goodman was born in Cornwall, UK and studied at Southampton University for a BSc in Pharmacology and a PhD in Applied Sciences. He has worked as both a postdoctoral researcher in genetics and editor of biomedical literature. He now lives in the heart of Europe in Brussels with his wife.

Epigraph

'For this world is not our permanent
home; we are looking forward to a home
yet to come.' (Heb 13:14)

Contents

Introduction

Our Father has written many messages to us in the past. His earnest desire is to communicate truths to us all that will aid, comfort and inspire our lives. If we listen carefully we will hear them and ours will be the greatest benefit. The *Letters* that follow are an arrangement and compilation of these messages; key verses of the Bible have been carefully paraphrased into the first person and written as our Father's direct instruction to us.

From the Bible we believe certain things about God, the world, man, sin, salvation, the church and the future. However, the unique nature by which the Bible was written means that these essential themes of Christianity do not flow sequentially but, as an early church theologian once said, 'God gives us truth in single threads, which we must weave into a finished texture'. By doing so, complete teachings on each of these areas of faith emerge and, as the Bible is the Word of God and inspired by Him, these *Letters* are our Father's personal message to us, His beloved children.

Each *Letter* focuses on a distinct area of Christian faith and gathers together the Scriptural verses that concern the set of beliefs. The central message of the Bible is of God's love to His people, and the theme running through each book of both the Old and New Testament is the plan of salvation, the way we can enter into a living and loving relationship with God. In every area of theology you can't help but to return to this same theme and this is why the gospel message is woven into each of the *Letters*; it is of central importance and everything else is secondary. Our Father wants us to know and live with Him, to enter His family whilst we are on this earth and afterwards to come home where we belong.

The first seven *Letters* are personally written for those who are still searching for God, for those who have not found their way to the Father. They point to Christ, our only Way to come to God and from the eighth *Letter* onwards it is assumed that the reader has accepted Christ into their life as the only remedy for our separation from God and has become His true child. In this way both the entreaties to be reconciled to Him and the intimate instructions to His children, such as the call to do His work, the gifts He gives and the precious promises of a glorious future are expressed with a gentle, personal and simple clarity.

By reading these *Letters from Home* you may readily understand many of the truths behind our faith. Each paraphrased verse from the Bible is clearly referenced, allowing you to study its original context in more depth. To further aid your study, an index of all the verses used can be found at the end of this book. The index shows the *Letter* in which it is used and some technical terms for the categories of theology which the *Letter* is mainly concerned with. This will be of help to the reader who studies theology at an advanced level and also to everyone who desires to study God's word in more depth through group or home study.

Writing this book has already blessed me in so many ways. I have had the opportunity to focus my attention on studying God's Word and a number of excellent theological texts. As this is also the first book I have written I have learnt many lessons in discipline and prayer. I have been humbled and at times this project seemed to be an impossible task, but I now know that everything is possible if we work alongside God. Theology, the Queen of the sciences, has always been interesting, absorbing and exciting to me and it is my hope that you too will experience the passion that can be found in this endeavour. It is my joy to offer these messages to the world and my prayer that they may help you understand what our Father is lovingly telling us in the Bible.

Neil Goodman
Brussels, September 2006

A key to abbreviated Bible references

The following *Letters* use the format of abbreviations shown below to indicate where the original Bible verse can be found.

OLD TESTAMENT

Gen	Genesis
Exod	Exodus
Lev	Leviticus
Num	Numbers
Deut	Deuteronomy
Josh	Joshua
Judg	Judges
Ruth	Ruth
1 Sam	1 Samuel
2 Sam	2 Samuel
1 Kgs	1 Kings
2 Kgs	2 Kings
1 Chr	1 Chronicles
2 Chr	2 Chronicles
Ezra	Ezra
Neh	Nehemiah
Esth	Esther
Job	Job
Ps	Psalms
Prov	Proverbs
Eccl	Ecclesiastes
Song	Song of Songs
Isa	Isaiah
Jer	Jeremiah
Lam	Lamentations
Ezek	Ezekiel
Dan	Daniel
Hos	Hosea
Joel	Joel
Amos	Amos
Obad	Obadiah
Jonah	Jonah
Mic	Micah
Nah	Nahum

Hab	Habakkuk
Zeph	Zephaniah
Hag	Haggai
Zech	Zechariah
Mal	Malachi

NEW TESTAMENT

Matt	Matthew
Mark	Mark
Luke	Luke
John	John
Acts	Acts
Rom	Romans
1 Cor	1 Corinthians
2 Cor	2 Corinthians
Gal	Galatians
Eph	Ephesians
Phil	Philippians
Col	Colossians
1 Thess	1 Thessalonians
2 Thess	2 Thessalonians
1 Tim	1 Timothy
2 Tim	2 Timothy
Titus	Titus
Philem	Philemon
Heb	Hebrews
Jas	James
1 Pet	1 Peter
2 Pet	2 Peter
1 John	1 John
2 John	2 John
3 John	3 John
Jude	Jude
Rev	Revelation

1   A Little About Me

My Dear Child,

I am your God, apart from Me there is no
    other; (Deut 4:35)
I am one God and Father of all creation,
    (Eph 4:6)
I have always been here; (Ps 93:2)
Before the mountains were made, before
    the universe was created,
I am always your everlasting God.
    (Ps 90:2)
You can rely on Me for I am eternal
    (Gen 21:33)
And I will always remain the same.
    (Ps 102:27)

My child, I am the King eternal. I am
    immortal and invisible. (1 Tim 1:17)
No one has ever seen Me, (John 1:18)
But Jesus, My only begotten Son,
    (John 3:16)
Has revealed Me throughout history.
    (John 1:18)
You can get to know Me by knowing Him
    (John 17:3)

For He continuously reveals Me to My
children. (John 17:26)

As My child, you will one day see My
face; (Ps 17:15)

Blessed indeed are those of you who are
pure in heart,

For you will see Me. (Matt 5:8)

For this reason you should try your very
hardest

To live peacefully with everyone and to be
holy;

For without holiness no one will see Me.
(Heb 12:14)

I am the living God; (Josh 3:10)

I have feelings and the power to do
whatever pleases Me. (Ps 115:3)

I am a person with self-consciousness, for
I am who I am. (Exod 3:14)

I stand alone – there is no one who rivals
Me, (Job 23:13)

No one can measure the extent of My
thoughts; (Ps 139:17–18)

There is no one on earth who completely
understands Me (Job 11:7)

For I am incomparable to anyone or
anything you may know. (Isa 40:18)

But it is My pleasure to explain the
mystery of My desires, (Eph 1:9)

For I am compassionate and gracious,

Slow to anger,

The Holder of love in all abundance.
(Ps 103:8)

Through My compassion

I made sure that My wonders would be
    remembered throughout history;
    (Ps 111:4)

I inspired books to be written for future
    ages,

For generations not yet created. (Ps 102:18)

From the most ancient of times I have
    made known My purpose

And what will happen in the end.
    (Isa 46:10)

I have a panoramic view of time;

Do not forget, for Me, eternity is one
    everlasting present

And a day is like a thousand years.
    (2 Pet 3:8)

For Me, a thousand years are like a day
    that has just passed, (Ps 90:4)

Therefore, do not worry. (Matt 6:34)

My eyes are everywhere,

Keeping watch on the wicked and the
    good (Prov 15:3)

And I have seen your tears. (Isa 38:5)

I have seen when you are miserable and I
    have heard you crying;

I am concerned about your suffering.
    (Exod 3:7)

My heart has been filled with pain for
    your condition from the beginning,
    (Gen 6:6)

For I can see you always. (Gen 16:13)

I know what is essential for your daily
    lives (Matt 6:32)

Therefore, do not be overly concerned for
    tomorrow,

Each day has its own share of difficulties.
(Matt 6:34)

Simply look for Me and My rule on earth
and

Your daily needs will be given to you.
(Matt 6:33)

I do not live in any one particular place
for I am Spirit –

Where I am, there is freedom. (2 Cor 3:17)

The whole universe cannot contain Me,
(1 Kgs 8:27)

I fill both heaven and earth. (Jer 23:24)

This is why I can be your perfect refuge
and strength,

For I am always present to help you.
(Ps 46:11)

If you call on Me in truth, I will be near
to you. (Ps 145:18)

Indeed, each time you pray,

I am closer to you than you can imagine.
(Deut 4:7)

Nothing in all creation is hidden from My
sight. (Heb 4:13)

I know you better than you know
yourself, My child, (Ps 139:3–7)

For I created the hearts of all and I consider
everything you do. (Ps 33:13–15)

I see all your ways and I examine every
path you choose to take. (Prov 5:21)

Both My Son – the Christ – and Our Holy
Spirit

Have been with Me from all eternity

And they too are God. (John 1:1–2;
Gen 1:2)

We know each other intimately and
    perfectly;

Indeed, you cannot come to know Me
    unless My Son reveals Me to you.

No one completely knows the Son except
    His Father, (Matt 11:27)

And My Holy Spirit knows the deepest
    parts of Me. (1 Cor 2:11)

I too know the mind of the Spirit

For the Spirit tells me everything,

Including all My children's needs and
    desires. (Rom 8:27)

I reveal Myself to you by My Spirit, He
    searches everything –

From the universe to My own deepest
    thoughts. (1 Cor 2:10)

This is how it should be, for who else
    knows your thoughts

Except your own self, your own spirit
    within you? (1 Cor 2:11)

Be strengthened for I am all-powerful, able
    to do anything I desire, (Job 23:13)

No plan of Mine can be thwarted;
    (Job 42:2)

For Me, all things are possible.
    (Matt 19:26)

Remember, it is I who made the entire
    universe,

Nothing is too difficult for Me. (Jer 32:17)

But some things are contrary to My
    nature:

My eyes are too pure to gaze on evil, I
    cannot tolerate wrong; (Hab 1:13)

I cannot deny Myself so I will always be
    faithful to you; (2 Tim 2:13)

I do not tempt anyone with evil and no
    evil can tempt Me; (Jas 1:13)

And I cannot lie,

My promises to you are true from before
    the beginning of time. (Titus 1:2)

You can therefore put your trust in Me

Because it is impossible for Me to lie.
    (Heb 6:18)

My child, trust in Me forever; (Isa 26:4)

Trust in Me with all your heart

And do not rely on your own
    understanding,

Acknowledge Me in everything you do

And I will guide you throughout life.
    (Prov 3:5–6)

You were made in My image, and
    (Gen 1:26)

I have sustained you since your birth.
    (Isa 46:3)

You exist, live and move within Me
    (Acts 17:28)

And, even to your old age, when your
    hair has become grey,

I will still be He who sustains you;

I have made you and I will always carry
    you and rescue you. (Isa 46:4)

Therefore, do not worry,

Entrust your cares to Me and I will
    support you; (Ps 55:22)

I care for you deeply, cast all your
    anxieties onto Me. (1 Pet 5:7)

You can be sure that I will not change; I,
    your Father, do not change. (Mal 3:6)

My love has always been with My
    children,

From everlasting to everlasting.
    (Ps 103:17)

My character remains the same and My
    years will never end. (Ps 102:27)

Although the heavens will be changed like
    a piece of clothing,

Like a robe I shall one day roll them up,

I will forever remain the same true God.
    (Heb 1:12)

Be therefore strengthened in your faith,

I have the power to fulfil all My promises
    to you. (Rom 4:21)

No matter how many promises I have
    made throughout history and before,

I want you to see that they are all 'Yes' in
    My Son Jesus. (2 Cor 1:20)

I have kept My promises because I am
    righteous; (Neh 9:8)

Righteousness and justice are My throne's
    foundation,

Love and faithfulness go before Me always.
    (Ps 89:14)

I am good, (Mark 10:18)

I am just, (2 Chr 12:6)

I am light. (1 John 1:5)

Look to Me and I will give you your daily
    needs, (Matt 6:11)

For the desires of every living creature are
    satisfied from My hand. (Ps 145:16)

I long for you. (Job 14:15)

Discover what pleases Me and live as a
child of light. (Eph 5:8–10)

Turn to Me and be saved. (Isa 45:22)

If you love My Son Jesus,

We will come and make Our home with
you. (John 14:23)

Because you will be My child,

I will send the very Spirit of My Son into
your heart. (Gal 4:6)

And, even if you have times of
faithlessness, I will remain faithful

For I cannot disown Myself. (2 Tim 2:13)

I will forever be Father to you and you
will be My child, (2 Cor 1:21–22)

No one will snatch you away from Me.
(John 10:29)

Love, your Father,
Almighty God

2 I Created You and All You See

My Dear Child,

I want you to understand that I created
the universe,

The heavens and the earth and everything
in them. (Acts 14:15)

For every building you see has an
architect and was built by someone,

But I am the Builder of everything there
is. (Heb 3:4)

Can you understand My mysteries?
(Job 11:7)

I perform wonders beyond your
understanding

And miracles you would not be able to
count. (Job 9:10)

You must realise that the universe came
into existence at My command.
(Heb 11:3)

I spoke and it happened, I ordered and it
was made; (Ps 33:6)

All that you can see did not exist before I
created it. (Heb 11:3)

At night, when you look up,

The stars declare the glories of My
handiwork.

Night after night, day after day, the skies
declare their knowledge

And speak of My work in a language that
everyone can understand. (Ps 19:1-3)

Lift your eyes, look at the stars – I created
all of these!

I know each of their names and by My
strength they continue to exist.
(Isa 40:26)

I stretched out the heavens and designed
the Plough, the Pleiades, Orion

And all the other constellations.
(Job 9:8–9)

I founded the earth by wisdom (Prov 3:19)

And suspended it in a vacuum. (Job 26:7)

I laid the foundations of the earth,
(Ps 102:25)

And covered it with the oceans as with a
piece of clothing. (Ps 104:6)

The earth is filled with My love.
(Ps 119:64)

Through My Son all things were made;
(John 1:3)

By My Spirit the breath of life was given.
(Gen 2:7)

The earth is full of My creatures;
(Ps 104:24)

When I send My Spirit, they are created.
(Ps 104:30)

I did not create the earth for it to be
empty (Isa 45:18)

But, by My will, I created all life on earth.
(Rev 4:11)

I am the Source and Support of
everything alive;

Within Me is the fountain of life. (Ps 36:9)

In My hand is the life of every creature

And the very breath of mankind.
(Job 12:10)

Consider what I have done, for great are
My works. (Ps 111:2)

Study the animals and you will learn,

Or the birds of the air, let them teach you;

Investigate the earth and you will know,

Or consider the fish of the sea and they
will inform you,

All these know that it was I who made
everything there is. (Job 12:7–9)

I caused the land to produce vegetation,
(Gen 1:11)

And the seas and skies to be filled with
creatures. (Gen 1:20)

Then, I blessed them and encouraged
them to fill the earth. (Gen 1:22)

I formed mankind from the elements of
the earth, (Gen 2:7)

And breathed life itself into you. (Job 33:4)

My child, know that it is I who made you,
that you are all My people. (Ps 100:3)

I give all men their life, breath and
everything else; (Acts 17:25)

I give life to every creature. (Neh 9:6)

From one man I have made every nation
of men. (Acts 17:26)

At the beginning of their creation, I made
   them male and female (Mark 10:6)

And determined when they should be
   born and where they should live.
   (Acts 17:26)

I created everyone so each would seek Me;

If you reach out for Me, you will find Me

For I am not far from you. (Acts 17:27)

I made you and shaped you like clay.
   (Job 10:8–9)

I created your innermost being

And knit you together in the womb of
   your mother; (Ps 139:13)

I poured you out like milk, curdled you
   like cheese

And clothed you with your body.
   (Job 10:10–11)

You were not hidden from Me for a
   moment;

I saw your unformed body and knew all
   the days of your life,

Even before one of them came to pass.
   (Ps 139:15–16)

I gave you your life, My child, and
   showed you kindness. (Job 10:12)

I knew you even before you were in the
   womb; (Jer 1:5)

You can rely on Me, for it was I who
   brought you forth into the world.
   (Ps 71:6)

I formed and made everyone for My
   glory. (Isa 43:7)

There is no favouritism with Me.
   (Acts 10:34)

Because, before Me, everyone is the same –
I have made you all as if from clay.
    (Job 33:6)

Do not be afraid, My child,
I know how you are formed and I
    remember that you are but dust,
Made of elements of the earth; (Ps 103:14)
I will not let you be tempted beyond what
    you can bear. (1 Cor 10:13)
For a little while you may have to suffer
    all kinds of trials, (1 Pet 1:6)
But look to Me and I will be your
    strength and your song, (Exod 15:2)
I know how to rescue you. (2 Pet 2:9)
Your time is short on this earth and your
    days are few. (Eccl 6:12)
So remember your Creator when you are
    young. (Eccl 12:1)

Your body returns to the dust of the earth
    from where it came
And your spirit returns to Me, who gave
    it. (Eccl 12:7)
Love Me with all your heart, soul,
    strength and mind; (Luke 10:27)
Trust in Me and I will save you,
    (Jer 39:18)
Not a hair on your head will be harmed,
    (Luke 21:18)
For I will be your Father and you will be
    My sons and daughters. (2 Cor 6:18)
My love and truth will forever protect
    you. (Ps 40:11)

Do not be discouraged,
I will never leave you nor abandon you.
   (Deut 31:8)

Love, your Father,
Almighty God

3 I am in Control

My Dear Child,

You were predestined and chosen by Me;
In the end, everything conforms to My
    will. (Eph 1:11)
I watch all mankind;
I, who crafted the hearts of everyone,
    consider everything you do.
    (Ps 33:14–15)

I am your Father and your God,
I strengthen mankind even though some
    do not acknowledge Me. (Isa 45:5)
I cause My sun to rise on both the good
    and the bad,
And rain to fall on the worthy and
    unworthy alike. (Matt 5:45)
I am patient with you. I do not want
    anyone to perish,
But for everyone to turn to Me. (2 Pet 3:9)
I show you kindness by sending rain from
    heaven,
Food for your body and joy for your
    heart. (Acts 14:17)

My Son Jesus is My radiant glory, the
  exact expression of My very nature;
By His own word He holds the universe
  together. (Heb 1:3)
I am behind the natural processes of this
  universe,
I know the laws of the heavens.
  (Job 38:33)
I cause the sun to rise, (Matt 5:45)
The wind to blow, (Ps 147:18)
And the rain and snow to fall. (Job 37:6)
I cut a path for the thunderstorm,
And send the lightning on its way.
  (Job 38:35)
I keep the beautiful Pleiades in place
And bring out the constellations in their
  seasons. (Job 38:31–32)

I rule over every nation on earth.
  (Ps 22:28)
I make countries great and reduce others;
I enlarge them and can disperse them.
  (Job 12:23)
Rulers are removed, I have lifted the
  humble to their thrones; (Luke 1:52)
I demote some and exalt others. (Ps 75:7)
I can deprive the leaders of their reason.
  (Job 12:24)
I bring one down and lift another up.
  (Ps 75:7)
I watch the nations and rule forever.
  (Ps 66:7)
I send both poverty and wealth; I both
  humble and exalt.
For the foundations of this earth are Mine,

Upon these I have built the world.
  (1 Sam 2:7–8)
Is it not right for Me to do what I wish
  with My own? (Matt 20:15)

Every nation's leaders should be wise and
  recognise My rule,
Be warned and seek My will. (Ps 2:10)
The governments that exist have been
  established by Me,
So everyone should obey them. (Rom 13:1)
But judge for yourselves whether their
  orders conflict with My law, (Acts 4:19)
For you must obey your God over men.
  (Acts 5:29)

I am always working; (John 5:17)
I am before all, holding everything
  together. (Col 1:17)
It is because of My mercy and love for
  you that you are not consumed.
  (Lam 3:22–23)
You lie down and sleep and wake again
  because I sustain you, (Ps 3:5)
So sleep in peace, My child, I grant sleep
  to those I love; (Ps 127:2)
I will keep you safe. (Ps 4:8)
Do not be deceived by anyone,
Every good and perfect gift you receive is
  from My hand. (Jas 1:16–17)

Do not worry about your life, (Matt 6:25)
Cast all your anxiety onto Me, for I care
  for you. (1 Pet 5:7)
I preserve both man and beast; (Ps 36:6)
I provide food for the cattle and the newly
  hatched birds. (Ps 147:9)

The lions roar and seek their food from
   Me, (Ps 104:21)

I feed the birds of the air, (Matt 6:26)

And the innumerable creatures of the sea
   look to Me for provision. (Ps 104:27)

Therefore, do not worry about how you
   will live;

As I feed everything else, so too will I care
   for you. (Matt 6:26)

Although all creation is wearing out, I
   will remain forever; (Ps 102:26–27)

All creation groans, waiting for the time
   when it will be refreshed.
   (Rom 8:21–22)

But it is still easier for the entire universe
   to disappear

Than for the smallest letter to be taken
   away from My law. (Luke 16:17)

For I am righteous and My law is right,
   (Ps 119:137)

My righteousness is everlasting and My
   law is true. (Ps 119:142)

The law springs from My eternal nature
   and is itself eternal,

This is why it cannot be broken.
   (Ps 119:160)

My law is written in the hearts and minds
   of everyone.

Your conscience sometimes condemns,
   sometimes defends you. (Rom 2:15)

This is My law; it is perfect and revives
   the soul. (Ps 19:7)

I wrote the natural laws of the universe,
   (Job 38:33)

And I am also the Author of its moral
laws. (Hos 8:12)

By these, everyone will be judged, (Ps 9:8)

Even those who do not know Me,

Because My law is instilled in their hearts.
(Rom 2:14–15)

Although the world is now chaotic and
dangerous,

With wars and rumours of wars,
(Matt 24:6)

I am still in control. (Lam 5:19)

All creation cries to Me, (Rom 8:22)

But, be assured, I will always be with My
children,

Even unto the end of the world.
(Matt 28:20)

I work for the good of those who love Me
(Rom 8:28)

And My love is eternally with them.
(Ps 103:17)

Nothing can separate them from the love
of Christ,

Neither trouble nor persecution, famine,
nakedness or danger. (Rom 8:35)

Be convinced that nothing in all creation –

Neither death nor life, angels or demons,

The present or the future, no height or
depth or any power –

Can separate My children from the love
revealed in My Son,

Jesus Christ, your Lord. (Rom 8:38–39)

Love, your Father,
Almighty God

4 Your Disobedient Condition

My Dear Child,

This world has turned away from Me.
(Rom 3:12)

I reared children and brought them up,
but everyone has turned against Me.
(Isa 1:2)

I was their Father, the very One who
made them.

But you have all acted corruptly towards
Me;

To your shame you are no longer My
children,

But a warped and deceitful generation.
(Deut 32:5–6)

If you say you have no sin, you lie to
yourselves, (1 John 1:8)

Everything you do seems right in your
eyes,

But I know your motives. (Prov 21:2)

You no longer know how to do right.
(Amos 3:10)

You do not understand what you do,

For when you want to do right, you do
    not do it. (Rom 7:15)

Even if you have the desire to do good,
    you are not able. (Rom 7:18)

Indeed, the spirit may be willing, but
    your body is weak. (Matt 26:41)

The whole world has become a prisoner of
    sin, (Gal 3:22)

And those who are controlled by their
    sinful nature cannot please Me.
    (Rom 8:8)

By your own free will, you have gone
    astray,

Each of you has turned to his own way.
    (Isa 53:6)

You have all fallen short of My glory.
    (Rom 3:23)

Even from your very birth, you tell lies
    and do not follow Me. (Ps 58:3)

People are boastful, proud, abusive,
    ungrateful, unholy,

Disobedient to their parents and are lovers
    of themselves and of money.
    (2 Tim 3:2)

You have all lived like this at one time,

Gratifying your cravings and following
    selfish motives, (Eph 2:3)

But I cannot stand these things.
    (Deut 25:16)

Even so, I gave you over to your
    shameful lusts, (Rom 1:24)

And let every nation of people go their
    own way. (Acts 14:16)

Everyone has eaten more than enough,

For I have given you what you craved.
    (Ps 78:29)

People have not even thought it
worthwhile to keep the knowledge of
Me,

So I gave you all over to a depraved mind.
(Rom 1:28)

You have a darkened understanding;

You are separated from My life because of
your ignorance, (Eph 4:18)

Separated by your sins, (Isa 59:2)

By the hardening of your hearts.
(Eph 4:18)

People go from bad to worse,

Deceiving others and deceiving
themselves. (2 Tim 3:13)

Having lost their sensitivity, people have
surrendered to sensuality,

With a continual lust for more. (Eph 4:19)

Although people know what is right and
wrong,

They not only do wrong but also approve
of others who sin. (Rom 1:32)

People are dead in their sins. (Eph 2:1)

Nothing good lives in your sinful nature,

For you may desire to do good, but you
cannot go through with it. (Rom 7:18)

The evil things you do delude and entrap
you,

The cords of your sin hold you captive.
(Prov 5:22)

This mind of sinful man is hostile to Me
and death to them,

But the Spirit-filled mind is life and peace.
(Rom 8:6–7)

The mind of the sinful man is set on the
desires of the sinful nature,

But the Spirit-filled mind is set on the
    Spirit's desires. (Rom 8:5)

I hate it when you plot against your
    neighbour,
And love to tell lies. (Zech 8:17)
Love does no harm to anyone,
Therefore love is the fulfilment of the law.
    (Rom 13:10)
My law is perfect. (Ps 19:7)
I will judge every deed, everything hidden,
Whether it is good or bad. (Eccl 12:14)
Those who reject the truth and are self-
    seeking,
These will bear My anger. (Rom 2:8)

In the past, I overlooked everyone's
    ignorance,
But now I command everyone to turn
    back to Me. (Acts 17:30)
Although My eyes are too pure to look on
    evil, (Hab 1:13)
My arm is not too short to save you.
    (Isa 59:1)
Because of the great love I have for you,
You can be saved. (Eph 2:4–5)
Because I love you all so much, I gave My
    one and only Son. (John 3:16)
I have demonstrated My love for you,
For while you were still sinning, Jesus
    died for you. (Rom 5:8)
He came that you may have life and have
    it more abundantly; (John 10:10)
If you but believe in Him you shall not
    perish but have everlasting life
    (John 3:16)

And sin shall no longer be your master.
    (Rom 6:14)

I am your King, your Lawgiver and your
    Judge;
It is I who will save you. (Isa 33:22)

Love, your Father,
Almighty God

5 *We have been Reconciled, Turn to Me*

My Dear Child,

I want to reveal and explain everything to
  you. (1 Cor 2:10)
My secret wisdom has been hidden in ages
  past (1 Cor 2:7)
And nobody had seen or heard what I
  have prepared for you, (1 Cor 2:9)
But My Spirit will teach you, (1 Cor 2:13)
And I will reveal Myself to you. (Isa 65:1)
I will open your eyes so that you may see
  wonderful things. (Ps 119:18)

Although you do not know how to do
  right, (Amos 3:10)
Realise that My kindness enables you to
  turn to Me; (Rom 2:4)
United with My Son Jesus you can be
  forgiven of your sins. (Eph 1:7)
I love My Son and have placed everything
  in His hands. (John 3:35)
He has destroyed death and brought life
  and immortality to light. (2 Tim 1:10)
My child, if you receive My Son into your
  life,

You become the very child of Almighty
    God. (John 1:12)

The wages of sin is death,

But My gift to you is everlasting life in
    union with My Son. (Rom 6:23)

I created you and gave you life.
    (Job 10:12)

I invite you now to be partners with My
    Son in a wonderful friendship,
    (1 Cor 1:9)

For at present we are separated by your
    sin. (Isa 59:2)

I want you to be with Me, My child –
    (John 17:24)

Turn away from your sin and all heaven
    will rejoice. (Luke 15:7)

Now is the time,

Today you can be saved. (2 Cor 6:2)

By My loving kindness, I have shown
    salvation to all men. (Titus 2:11)

For every living soul belongs to Me,

Both parent and child. (Ezek 18:4)

As My moral law was powerless to save
    you,

Weakened as it was by your sinful nature,

I sent My own Son in the likeness of a
    sinful man to be your sacrifice.
    (Rom 8:3)

My law guided and directed you to Him
    and,

As faith has now come to you,

You are no longer watched over by the
    law. (Gal 3:24–25)

Understand, My child, you are justified by
your faith,

Not by trying to follow strict rules.
(Rom 3:28).

My Son redeemed you from this curse of
the law

By becoming a curse for you. (Gal 3:13)

Anyone who has sinned has broken My
moral law,

But Jesus has come to take away your
sins. (1 John 3:4–5)

I made Him who had no sin to be your sin,

So that you may be made blameless
before Me. (2 Cor 5:21)

For My Son did not come into this world
to be served,

But to give His life in payment for you.
(Mark 10:45)

He bore your sins in His body,

So that you might die to sin and live for
good. (1 Pet 2:24)

Understand, My child, that at the right
time,

When you were powerless, (Rom 5:6)

Christ died for your sins once and for all
time to bring you to Me. (1 Pet 3:18)

He gave Himself to redeem you, to buy
you back,

To purify you so you could become His
very own. (Titus 2:14)

For if you walk in the light with Jesus,

His sacrificed blood purifies you from all
sin. (1 John 1:7)

Jesus died for you all so that you should
no longer live for yourselves,

But for Him. (2 Cor 5:15)

Whoever has My Son has life itself,
(1 John 5:12)

But he who does not believe stands
condemned. (John 3:18)

Whoever believes in My Son has life
everlasting,

But he who rejects My Son must endure
My anger. (John 3:36)

Humble yourselves, therefore, and I will
lift you up; (Jas 4:10)

If you confess your sins, I will be faithful
to forgive and purify you. (1 John 1:9)

You will gain access to My grace by faith,
(Rom 5:2)

For through My Son Jesus you have
access to your Father,

By the one Spirit. (Eph 2:18)

Therefore, My child,

As you have confidence to enter the holiest
of places by His blood, (Heb 10:19)

Draw near to Me, draw near with a
sincere heart

And with the full assurance of faith.
(Heb 10:22)

Sin shall no longer be your master, for
you are no longer under law,

But under My grace. (Rom 6:14)

When He died, He died to sin once and for
all time;

In the same way, consider yourself dead
to sin

But alive to Me, in My Son Christ Jesus.
(Rom 6:10–11)

You were once controlled by your sinful nature,

But by dying to what kept you prisoner, you have been released

And serve in the new way of the Spirit.
(Rom 7:5–6)

Disregard your former way of life, your old self

And be renewed in the spirit of your mind.

Clothe yourself with your new nature,

Created in the fashion of My holiness.
(Eph 4:22–24)

Anyone who does not have My Spirit

Does not accept anything that is from My Spirit;

It is stupidity to him and he cannot understand it. (1 Cor 2:14)

This message appears to be foolishness to those who will not listen

But to you who are being saved, it is My own great power. (1 Cor 1:18)

These things are hidden from the conceited,

But I am contented to reveal them to little children, (Matt 11:25–26)

Heaven itself belongs to such as these.
(Matt 19:14)

In all honesty, My child, if you hear and believe Me

You have eternal life – you have passed over from death to life. (John 5:24)

This faith I have given you as a gift

And through this faith you are saved.
(Eph 2:8)

No one who denies My Son has Me,

But whoever accepts Him has Me also.
(1 John 2:23)

When you believe, you receive My Holy
Spirit. (Eph 1:13)

There is no longer any condemnation for
those in My Son; (Rom 8:1)

I condemned the sin in you,

Now the righteousness of My law may be
achieved in you. (Rom 8:3–4)

At the end of time, angels will come

And separate the ungodly from the
righteous. (Matt 13:49)

I will not forsake My faithful ones;

I will protect them forever. (Ps 37:28)

But the wicked, those who call evil good
and good evil,

Those who substitute light for darkness,
(Isa 5:20)

These will be cut off, (Ps 37:28)

They will go to eternal punishment,
(Matt 25:46)

For the sting of death is sin, (1 Cor 15:56)

But the righteous will go to eternal life.
(Matt 25:46)

The cross has put an end to any hostility
between us. (Eph 2:15–16)

When He made peace through His blood
shed on the cross,

All things, whether on earth or in heaven,
were reconciled; (Col 1:20)

He nailed your very own debt to the
cross. (Col 2:14)

My Son did away with sin once and
forever. (Heb 9:26–27)

Therefore, if you are in My Son,

You are a new creation – all things have
been transformed. (2 Cor 5:17)

My children shall live by their faith,
(Rom 1:17)

And through faith you can approach Me
freely and confidently. (Eph 3:12)

Therefore stand before Me with boldness

And obtain My mercy and help in times
of need. (Heb 4:16)

By My grace you have been saved

By your faith, which I have given you.
(Eph 2:8)

I showed My grace to you,

And brought with it salvation for all.
(Titus 2:11)

Come near to Me, My child, and I will
come near to you.

Be pure in all your thoughts, motives and
deeds; (Jas 4:8)

Love Me, and I and My Son will make
Our home with you. (John 14:23)

Love, your Father,
Almighty God

6 My Son, the Christ

My Dear Child,

I am writing so that you may believe that
   Jesus is my Son;
By believing this you can have everlasting
   life
In His wonderful name. (John 20:31)

Out of My love,
I will forever encourage you and give you
   hope. (2 Thess 2:16)
To save you from your sins,
I sent My Son. (1 John 4:10)
He who was without sin
Came to earth to take away your sins.
   (1 John 3:5)
He came to do My will. (Heb 10:7)

As My dear children are human, made of
   flesh and blood,
My Son also shared in the same.
   (Heb 2:14)
He did not become a sinful man, but its
   very likeness,
So He could be your sacrifice for sin

And truly destroy the sin within you all.
  (Rom 8:3)
He came to remove all your sins.
  (1 John 3:5)

My Son has come into the world,
  (John 11:27)
But do you know who He is, My child?
  (Matt 22:42)
He is My firstborn, superior over all
  creation; (Col 1:15)
He has been with Me from before the
  beginning, (1 John 2:13)
And through Him all things have been
  created,
Nothing exists that has not been made by
  Him. (John 1:3)

He is the Alpha and the Omega,
  (Rev 22:13)
The First and the Last. (Rev 1:17)
He is Wonderful, Counsellor,
Prince of Peace (Isa 9:6)
And Lord of all. (Acts 10:36)
The Holy One, (John 6:69)
The Word, (John 1:1)
Your Lord and your God. (John 20:28)

His name is above all other names,
  (Phil 2:9)
For He is the Holy and Righteous One.
  (Acts 3:14)

He came into the world to save you,
  (1 Tim 1:15)
And to bring you home to Me.
  (John 14:2–3)

For He alone is the Way to Me;

He alone is the Truth and the Life.
(John 14:6)

He is God over all (Rom 9:5)

And My very own Son – listen to Him!
(Matt 17:5)

Some thought Him to be a mere man
(John 10:33)

And some still do,

For there are many who do not believe
that the Christ has come. (2 John 1:7)

They try to deceive even My chosen ones
– if that were possible. (Matt 24:24)

No, in Christ, the fullness of My nature
lives in the form of a man. (Col 2:9)

He is the very image of Myself (Col 1:15)

And perfectly represents Me in all ways.
(Heb 1:3)

When you really know Jesus,

You will also know Me. (John 14:7)

He knows all things, (John 21:17)

For in Him are great treasures:

Hidden wisdom and knowledge. (Col 2:3)

He is,

And was,

And is to come, He is the Almighty,
(Rev 1:8)

We are One. (John 17:11)

My Son has true humility,

For, although He had the very nature of
God

And was like Me in every way,

He did not cling to His rights,

Demanding to keep this equality (Phil 2:6)

But My Divine Word, My one and only Son,

Became man and lived among you.

He left My side so that you may see His glory. (John 1:14)

He emptied Himself and became like nothing, He took a servant's nature

And was made human. (Phil 2:7)

My Son agreed to do My will: (Heb 10:9)

Although He was wealthy,

He became poor for you

So that through His poverty you may become rich! (2 Cor 8:9)

He shared the humanity of all My children (Heb 2:14)

And was directly descended from King David as I had promised. (Rom 1:3)

On earth, His father was known as Joseph (John 6:42)

And His mother's name was Mary. (Matt 13:55)

His childhood was in Nazareth (Luke 4:16)

And He was obedient to His parents. (Luke 2:51)

As the years passed He became strong (Luke 2:40)

And grew in wisdom, (Luke 2:52)

So much so that everyone was amazed at My Child. (Luke 2:47)

The Man that people knew from Nazareth,

Is the same Man that mediates between you and Me today. (1 Tim 2:5)

He can fully identify with you, because
(Heb 2:14)

He has also been tired, (John 4:6)

Thirsty, (John 19:28)

Hungry (Matt 4:2)

And tempted in every way. (Heb 4:15)

He can truly help you when you are
tempted,

For He too has suffered under temptation.
(Heb 2:18)

Come to Jesus, therefore, when you are
weary and burdened with troubles

And He will give you rest.

Learn from My Son and find rest for your
souls. (Matt 11:28–29)

I anointed My Son with My Holy Spirit

And was with Him on earth. (Acts 10:38)

He is gentle, with a humble heart,
(Matt 11:29)

And, everywhere He went, He did good

For I was with Him. (Acts 10:38)

His life on earth was one of prayer.
(Heb 5:7)

Jesus prayed alone on mountainsides;
(Matt 14:23)

He spent the night there, talking with Me.
(Luke 6:12)

Early in the morning, before it was yet
light,

He would rise and meet with Me.
(Mark 1:35)

He prayed hard and made requests with
tears, and

Out of His reverent submission,
I heard Him. (Heb 5:7)

He taught at dawn, and (John 8:2)
The very words He spoke were My own.
(John 14:24)
He was always passionate about doing
My work. (John 9:4)
He came and preached a message of peace
to all,
Both near and far,
For through Him, everyone can come to
Me. (Eph 2:17–18)

Whatever I do, My Son also does.
(John 5:19)
And He has told you what He saw when
He was in My company. (John 8:38)
It was through Him that I made the
universe. (Heb 1:2)

Follow My Son, My child, (John 8:12)
And you will surely live, even if you die,
for
He is the One who raises the dead and
gives them life, (John 11:25–26)
He is the Way to Me. (John 14:6)

You must understand, My child, He is the
way to your Father,
No one comes to Me except through Him.
(John 14:6)
Your salvation cannot be found in anyone
else. (Acts 4:12)

Jesus has become My wisdom for you,

Your holiness, righteousness and freedom
from sin's penalty. (1 Cor 1:30)

My child, take Jesus as your example,

And follow in His steps. (1 Pet 2:21)

If you say you live in Him, you must
walk as He did (1 John 2:6)

And speak as if they are the very words
of God. (1 Pet 4:11)

Do not have petty arguments,

Do not be resentful,

But be kind to everyone. (2 Tim 2:24)

Live a life of love My child. (Eph 5:2)

The secret knowledge of the Kingdom of
heaven I give to you, (Matt 13:11)

For Christ is My mystery,

Be therefore united in love and you will
have complete comprehension.
(Col 2:2–3)

For this joy, Jesus, My Author and
Perfecter of your faith,

Endured the shame of the cross –

Fix your sight on Him alone. (Heb 12:2)

I have told you all this so that you may
share in My joy; (John 15:11)

Fill your hearts, take My total joy within
you, (John 17:13)

That you may be complete. (John 15:11)

Love, your Father,
Almighty God

7 What My Son has Accomplished for You

My Dear Child,

I knew you would turn away from Me
So I planned ahead for it –
I chose Christ even before the creation of
    the world
To be the One to bring you back,
And I have now revealed Him to you.
    (1 Pet 1:20)

I gave orders to My Son, and
Sent Him with work He had to
    accomplish. (John 5:36)
Know, My child, that My Son loved Me,
    and
Did everything I asked Him. (John 14:31)

He has volunteered His life for everyone
    in the world. (John 6:51)
It is not because you loved Me that I sent
    My only Son,
But because I love you, so dearly.
    (1 John 4:10)

Through miracles, My Son revealed His
   glory to His disciples,
And they placed their faith in Him.
   (John 2:11)
My Son knew His mission was to die
And told all who were close to Him.
   (Matt 17:22)
He explained that His Father loved Him
And that He would lay down His life,
   only to take it up again. (John 10:17)
He instructed them to listen carefully, for
   He would be betrayed, (Luke 9:44)
He would be condemned to death
   (Matt 20:18)
And after three days He would rise to life.
   (Mark 9:31)
He told them He was returning to Me,
To His Father and to His God. (John 20:17)
But they did not understand Him.
   (Mark 9:32)

In His entire life, He never went against
   My will and never lied. (1 Pet 2:22)
Nobody could prove Him guilty of sin,
   (John 8:46)
Yet He suffered many things and was
   rejected by everyone. (Luke 17:25)

He was insulted, (Rom 15:3)
He was loathed and not accepted by men,
He was full of sorrows and no stranger to
   suffering. (Isa 53:3)
Yet when they gave their abuse,
He did not retaliate;
He suffered, but threatened no one,

For His trust was in the righteous Judge.
(1 Pet 2:23)

His soul was overwhelmed with sorrow,
(Matt 26:38)

For He carried your sins within Him, in
His body, (1 Pet 2:24)

And suffered in His soul. (Isa 53:11)

The punishment that was rightly yours
Fell on Him;
He was crushed to bring you peace, and
Through His wounds are healed.
(Isa 53:5)

He was betrayed for money, (Matt 26:15)
Just as it was written hundreds of years
before it happened. (Matt 27:9)
He was given to sinful men who crucified
Him,
But on the third day He beat death and
rose to life. (Mark 8:31)

They mocked Him on the cross saying,
'Save yourself if you can'.
(Luke 23:36–37)
But it was I who brought Him safely
from the womb;
From the earliest of times He has trusted
Me,
Even as a baby He knew Me as God
(Ps 22:9–10)
And Father. (Luke 2:49)
I would not hide My face from Him –
I heard His cry for help. (Ps 22:24)

He gave up His Spirit into My protection,
And breathed no more. (Luke 23:46)

My child, this is of supreme importance:

My Son died for you,

Just as it was predicted by My prophets
of old,

He was buried in a tomb, and I raised
Him to life on the third day,

Just as it was written,

And He was seen by many. (1 Cor 15:3–5)

The Author of life was killed, (Acts 3:15)

But I raised My Servant so you could be
blessed –

Turn from your sins, My child. (Acts 3:26)

By being lifted up on the cross, Jesus drew
everyone to Himself. (John 12:32)

On the third day, I raised My Son and
many saw Him. (Acts 10:40)

I raised My Son from the dead –
(1 Thess 1:10)

The First and the Last had died but was
risen to life, (Rev 2:8)

For death could not hold Him. (Acts 2:24)

His disciples saw the empty tomb,

But they didn't understand that He must
rise from the dead. (John 20:3–9)

On the Sunday after My Son's death,

His disciples were together with their
doors locked,

For they were afraid of what the people
outside might do.

But Jesus came to them, offering peace,
and they were overjoyed.
(John 20:19–20)

When they saw Him they were shocked
and afraid at first, (Luke 24:37)

Some were doubtful, (Matt 28:17)

But they looked at the holes in His hands
and feet (Luke 24:39)

And they remembered His words when He
taught them afresh. (Luke 24:7–8)

After which, they resolved to know
nothing except Christ

And Him crucified. (1 Cor 2:2)

They shared meals with Him after He had
risen, (Acts 10:41)

And He appeared to His disciples for forty
days,

Talking about My Kingdom. (Acts 1:3)

He was seen by more than 500 people at
the same time; (1 Cor 15:6)

There were many witnesses. (Acts 2:32)

I handed Him over to die for your offences,

But I raised Him to life to make you right
with Me. (Rom 4:25)

For if I had left My Son in the grave,

Your faith would be worthless and your
sins would remain. (1 Cor 15:17)

But I raised Him from among the dead

Freeing Him from the sorrow of death
(Acts 2:24)

And as I raised Christ, so will I raise you
to be with Me. (1 Cor 15:12–13)

He is the firstfruits of all who will die, for
all will be raised. (1 Cor 15:20)

You see, My child, Christ came once to
take away the sins of many,

And He will come again,

Bringing with Him salvation for all who
    wait for Him. (Heb 9:28)

When He is revealed from heaven,

He will relieve you of all your troubles.
    (2 Thess 1:7)

When Jesus returns everyone will see
    Him –

Even the very ones who pierced Him and
    hung Him on the cross. (Rev 1:7)

My children physically die and are buried
    along with their fathers, (Acts 13:36)

But I did not abandon My Holy One;

I could not let Him see decay. (Ps 16:10)

The people who travelled with Him
    during His life

Saw Him for many days. (Acts 13:31)

After this I took Him up into heaven,
    (Mark 16:19)

He ascended before their very eyes,
    (Eph 4:8)

Until a cloud hid Him and they could see
    Him no more. (Acts 1:9)

He is now present everywhere (Eph 4:10)

And sits at My right hand in the realms
    of heaven, (Eph 1:20)

Interceding on your behalf, pleading your
    case before Me. (Rom 8:34)

He now sits at a place of honour with Me.
    (Luke 22:69)

For, by His resurrection from the dead,

The Holy Spirit mightily declared that
    Jesus was My Son (Rom 1:4)

And all angels, authorities and powers have
    been made subject to Him. (1 Pet 3:22)

I have placed all things under His
    authority –

He is above all rule, power and title that
    can be given; (Eph 1:21–22)

I have made My Son both Lord and
    Christ. (Acts 2:36)

My child, regret your wrongdoings and
    change your ways,

Turn to Me that I may wipe out your sins
    and revive you. (Acts 3:19)

Turn to me, so I can send My Son again

For He cannot come until the appointed
    time. (Acts 3:20)

Through My kindness I try to lead you to
    repentance. (Rom 2:4)

My child, if you confess that Jesus is
    truly Lord,

And believe that I raised Him from the
    dead,

You will surely be saved. (Rom 10:9)

This message is silliness to those who will
    not listen,

But to My children being saved,

It is My own great power – (1 Cor 1:18)

It can rescue you from darkness

And bring you to My beloved Son's
    Kingdom. (Col 1:13)

Love, your Father,
Almighty God

8 My Holy Spirit, Your Counsellor

My Dear Child,

Jesus was conceived by My Holy Spirit
(Matt 1:18)
And by Him you were made. (Job 33:4)
He is everywhere;
There are no places kept secret from Him,
(Ps 139:7–10)
For He created the world. (Gen 1:2)

My Holy Spirit shows you and convicts
you of your wrongdoings, (John 16:8)
And works through your will to enable
you to turn to Me
So that My desires may become yours.
(Phil 2:13)

I saved you,
Not by anything good that you may have
done,
But out of My mercy –
You are saved by your rebirth and your
renewal,
Performed by My Spirit within you.
(Titus 3:5)

Some tried to dissuade My Son from
carrying out His work, (Matt 16:22)

But the truth is that it is better for
everyone that He went away,

For, when He left, He sent the Counsellor
to come to you. (John 16:7)

Jesus was baptized with water,

But He Himself baptizes you with the
Holy Spirit. (John 1:33)

By the one Spirit, (1 Cor 12:13)

All My children are born into My family,
(Heb 2:11)

And the same Spirit is given to all to
drink. (1 Cor 12:13)

For there is but one Lord,

One faith,

One baptism. (Eph 4:5)

Your Counsellor is the very Spirit of truth
that goes out from Me – (John 15:26)

Through Him the Scriptures were written,
and (2 Tim 3:16)

My Son has sent Him to you as a gift
from Me; (John 15:26)

I promised you the Spirit, and He has
poured Him out for you. (Acts 2:33)

When you turned to Me, My child,

I sent the very Spirit of My Son into your
heart; (Gal 4:6)

He will tell you all about Me (John 15:26)

For He is the Spirit of wisdom and
understanding. (Isa 11:2)

He will reveal Me in order for you to
know Me better. (Eph 1:17)

I give without limit and the words He will
    say are My own. (John 3:34)

My child, He will clothe you with My
    power, (Luke 24:49)
With robes of righteousness. (Rev 19:8)
For, by Him, you are reborn! (John 3:6–7)
My child, receive the Spirit of My Son,
    (John 20:22)
Receive His fire. (Matt 3:11)

I give the same gift of My Spirit to all
    who believe. (Acts 11:16–17)
And in the one Spirit there are many gifts.
    (1 Cor 12:4)

Know that I live in you
By My Spirit that I have freely given you.
    (1 Cor 2:12)
My Spirit in you sets you free from the
    sinful nature – (Rom 8:9)
He brings you freedom. (2 Cor 3:17)
For you are led by My Spirit
And are no longer under My law.
    (Gal 5:18)

You have My Spirit within you,
Given as a deposit guaranteeing that you
    are Mine. (Eph 1:14)
My Spirit testifies with your own,
In perfect agreement, We know that you
    are My child. (Rom 8:16)

He speaks only of what He hears
    (John 16:13)
And He knows My very thoughts.
    (1 Cor 2:11)

He will tell you what has yet to happen,

He will bring glory to My Son by
    revealing to you what is His,

For all that belongs to Me is His.
    (John 16:13–15)

You are very special,

For do you not know, My child, that you
    are My sacred dwelling place,

My holy temple? (1 Cor 3:16)

It is I, your God, that lives inside you,

You are not your own. (1 Cor 6:19)

My Son's own temple was destroyed,

But He raised it again in three days.
    (John 2:19)

My Spirit raised Christ from the dead,

And it is My same Spirit that now lives in
    you. (Rom 8:11)

My Spirit within you shows you belong
    to Christ,

And guarantees your wonderful future.
    (2 Cor 1:22)

Be filled with the Spirit and with wisdom.
    (Acts 6:3)

For if you do not have My Spirit, you do
    not belong to My Son. (Rom 8:9)

How can you recognise those with My
    Spirit?

If they acknowledge that Christ became
    human, (1 John 4:2)

That the Word became a man and lived
    among you, (John 1:14)

Then they are My children. (1 John 4:2)

Do not lie to Him, (Acts 5:3)

For He has sealed you to be with Me.
(Eph 4:30)

In the past, some have grieved Him

And so I turned away and fought against
them. (Isa 63:10)

There are always those who resist
(Acts 7:51)

And insult the grace of your God, My
Spirit. (Heb 10:29)

But let Me warn you:

I will not forgive people who speak evilly
against Him. (Matt 12:31)

Do not extinguish His fire within you.
(1 Thess 5:19)

With My Holy Spirit you have been sealed
and secured for the day of redemption,

Do not grieve Him. (Eph 4:30)

So why not live by My Spirit?

You will no longer be compelled to do
what is wrong,

For that is contrary to His ways.

But, if you are led by My Spirit

You will do what you desire most.
(Gal 5:16–18)

To be under the control of My Spirit is
both life and peace, (Rom 8:6)

An abundant life (John 10:10)

At peace with everyone. (Mark 9:50)

By My will, the Spirit intercedes for you,

He pleads your case before Me. (Rom 8:27)

In a language that words cannot describe,
He prays for you in your weakness;

When you have no idea what you need
(Rom 8:26)
The Spirit of My Son calls out for His
Father. (Gal 4:6)

He will teach you everything,
For He is your Counsellor; (John 14:26)
He will lay down wisdom deep within
you. (Ps 51:6)

As you trust in Me you will be filled with
joy and peace;
By the power of My Spirit you will
overflow with hope. (Rom 15:13)

He will open the meaning of the
Scriptures to you. (Luke 24:32)
Using spiritual words to explain spiritual
truths,
I will teach you through Him. (1 Cor 2:13)
From My anointing you will learn the
truth, (1 John 2:20)
Your anointing will teach you about
everything
So remain in Him; (1 John 2:27)
Let My Spirit rest on you, (Isa 11:2)
Let Him fill you completely. (Eph 5:18)

My child, you know that a tree is known
by its fruit. (Luke 6:44)
Know too that the fruit of the Spirit is
Love, joy, peace,
Patience, faithfulness and self-control.
(Gal 5:22–23)
Composed of all that is good, right and
true (Eph 5:9)

It comes through Jesus for My glory.
(Phil 1:11)

Bear much fruit, My child,

You can be sure that it will last.
(John 15:16)

When you are filled with My Spirit,

You may address the authorities, (Acts 4:8)

You may speak the word of God boldly
(Acts 4:31)

And you may even speak in other
languages; (Acts 2:4)

My Holy Spirit will give you the words to
say. (Luke 12:12)

He will set you apart for the work to
which He calls you. (Acts 13:2)

There are different types of work,

But I perform them all through My
children. (1 Cor 12:6)

As He chooses,

The Spirit gives gifts to each of My
children: (1 Cor 12:11)

If yours is serving, then serve
unreservedly;

If it is encouraging, encourage with all
your heart;

If it is helping, then give generously;

If it is showing mercy, then do so with a
smile;

If you are a leader, then govern carefully
and honestly;

And if your gift is prophesying, use it in
proportion to your faith. (Rom 12:6–8)

He gives some of My children to be
apostles,

Some to be teachers (Eph 4:11)

But, My child, you should use whatever
gift you have received

To serve others. (1 Pet 4:10)

For it is through you that We desire to
work. (Phil 2:13)

Love, your Father,
Almighty God

9 I Chose You to be in My Family, United with My Son

My Dear Child,

Do not be concerned that the rest of the world do not welcome My Gift.

They do not accept Him, because they cannot see or know Him;

But you know Him, My child,

For He lives in you and is with you.

You are not an orphan

Because the Spirit of My Son, the Counsellor, is with you.
(John 14:16–19)

Though your failures had separated you from Me,

Through Jesus, I have forgiven you;
(Acts 13:38)

You could not see Me because of your sins, (Isa 59:2)

But, My child, you were appointed for life everlasting. (Acts 13:48)

Like a sheep you were going astray,
  (1 Pet 2:25)
But the Good Shepherd laid down His life
  for you, (John 10:14–15)
And I brought Him back from the dead –
  He is the great Shepherd (Heb 13:20)
Of Our one flock. (John 10:16)

Put your hope in the Saviour of all men,
  the Living God. (1 Tim 4:10)
This faith I have given you, (Rom 12:3)
By this gift you are saved. (Eph 2:8)

I have chosen you. (1 Thess 1:4)
I knew how you would respond to Me
And so I planned for you to be changed,
To have My Son's likeness. (Rom 8:29)
I chose you to be My child (1 Thess 1:4)
And you turned to Me, just as I had
  decided beforehand; (Acts 4:28)
From before the beginning of time
I chose you to be without blame before
  Me. (Eph 1:4)

I work all things to happen for the good
  of My children, (Rom 8:28)
And I have chosen you as My child.
  (Eph 1:11)
This is My secret wisdom, the hidden
  wisdom I destined for your glory.
  (1 Cor 2:7)
For I have called you
And you are justified in My sight.
  (Rom 8:30)

From far away, you have been brought
    near; (Eph 2:13)

By My grace I enabled you to come to Me.
    (John 6:44)

Those I have given to My Son,

These are Mine. (John 17:9)

For I chose you in Him. (Eph 1:11)

I know everything you will ever do,
    (Ps 139:16)

And I chose you to be My child from the
    beginning of time. (2 Thess 2:13)

My Son has chosen you to work and bear
    fruit,

So I will give you whatever you ask for in
    His name. (John 15:16)

It was My great pleasure to plan your
    adoption

As My sons and daughters. (Eph 1:5)

I love you, My children,

For you love My Son and know that He is
    from Me. (John 16:27)

I lavish My love on you,

I call you My child, (1 John 3:1)

And called you to be in My family.
    (Rom 8:30)

You are in the same family as My Son –

Jesus Himself is not ashamed to call you
    His brothers and sisters! (Heb 2:11)

My children are everything to My Son –

They are His mother, brother and sister to
    Him, (Matt 12:49–50)

They hear His word and apply it in their
    lives. (Luke 8:21)

And as you are My child,
So you are also an heir; (Gal 4:7)
You have full rights as My child. (Gal 4:5)
All this is from Me, for
We are reconciled through Christ.
    (2 Cor 5:17–18)

I did not give you a spirit making you a
    slave to fear,
But the Spirit of adoption –
By Him you call out in truth to your
    Father. (Rom 8:15)

My daughters, your faith has made you
    whole, (Matt 9:22)
My sons, follow Me all your life, (Jer 3:19)
For, by the Holy Spirit you can cry out to
    Me –
Your true Dad, your one Father. (Rom 8:15)

My Holy Spirit works through your will
    to enable you
To turn to Me so that My desires become
    yours. (Phil 2:13)
Examine yourself, My child,
Do you know My Son within? (2 Cor 13:5)
He is in you, vitalizing your spirit
    through righteousness. (Rom 8:10)

You live in Him,
And He in you,
For He has given you His very Spirit.
    (1 John 4:13)

My Son is within you as you are in Him

And through Christ you are all within
    Me. (John 14:20)

Everyone led by My Spirit is My child.
    (Rom 8:14)

Stay in Me and I will stay in you.
    (John 15:4)

You have been crucified with Christ,
    (Gal 2:20)

Your old self with its body of sin was
    killed; (Rom 6:6)

You no longer live, but it is My Son
    within you (Gal 2:20)

And through union with Christ in His
    death,

Be assured you will also be united in His
    resurrection. (Rom 6:5)

This hope is My most glorious mystery:

We have made Our home with you.
    (John 14:23)

And I have given you My precious
    promises,

For you participate in My own divine
    nature,

Escaping the corruption of this world.
    (2 Pet 1:4)

By My Spirit you know that you live in
    My Son,

For I have given you His Spirit.
    (1 John 4:13)

You have united yourself in the Lord

And are spiritually one with Him.
    (1 Cor 6:17)

If you live in love, My child,
You will live in Me,
And I in you,
For I am Love. (1 John 4:16)

My Son gives eternal life to those I have
   given Him (John 17:2)
And reveals Me to you. (John 17:6)
Take My free gift of the water of life!
   (Rev 22:17)
This water will well up within you into a
   spring (John 4:14)
Benefiting you with holiness leading to
   life everlasting. (Rom 6:22)

I have given you to My Son.
Be assured, He will never drive you away.
   (John 6:37)
But if you choose not to stay in Him
You will be like a pruned branch that is
   thrown away,
For apart from Him you can achieve
   nothing. (John 15:5–6)

My Son is the Vine, you are the branches
   (John 15:5)
And I am the Gardener. (John 15:1)
You will bear much fruit if you stay in
   My Son
For He will remain in you. (John 15:5)
But every branch that does not bear fruit
   will be removed. (John 15:2)

I am your faithful God,
Your Rock, (Deut 32:4)

There is none like Me in all the world.
(Jer 10:7)

You are secure in My hand. (John 10:29)

My child, do you know that if you believe
in My Son

You will never die? (John 11:26)

Wait eagerly for your complete adoption
into My family,

Then your very bodies will be redeemed,
made new and free. (Rom 8:23)

All creation must hear the good news.
(Mark 16:15)

The work I call you to do is to

Trust and believe in the One I have sent.
(John 6:29)

Tell it everywhere,

To the very ends of the earth. (Acts 1:8)

Tell everyone I will be their Father

And they can be My sons and daughters.
(2 Cor 6:18)

Share in the glory of My Son,

Share in the good news. (2 Thess 2:14)

My child, walk as Jesus did, (1 John 2:6)

Walk in the Spirit,

As is fitting for My children. (Rom 8:14)

Believe in My Son and love each other,

Just as He commanded – (1 John 3:23)

There is work prepared for you to do.
(Eph 2:10)

Just as you carry the likeness of all men
on earth,

So too will you bear the likeness of My
    Son from heaven. (1 Cor 15:49)
With My Son's Spirit in your heart,
    (2 Cor 1:22)
People will see the good work you do
And, through you,
Praise Me. (Matt 5:16)

Love, your Father,
Almighty God

10 Separate and Dedicate Yourself to Me

My Dear Child,

I want you to be sanctified,
To set yourself apart for Me. (1 Thess 4:3)

Do not be like the rest of the world,
For you are no longer merely human.
  (1 Cor 3:3)
Give yourself to Me as both holy and
  pleasing:
This is true spiritual worship. (Rom 12:1)
Do everything in your power to live holy
  lives,
In peace with everyone. (Heb 12:14)

My child, you are being cleansed and
  made holy
By the washing of yourself with My
  Word, the Scriptures. (Eph 5:26)
Remove all things from your lives that
  pollute you, (2 Chr 29:5)
Make a decision to purify yourself from
  all bodily and spiritual contaminants

And do your best to perfect holiness out
    of love and respect for Me, (2 Cor 7:1)
Becoming like My very Son. (Rom 8:29)

Rid yourself of all bitterness and anger,
    fighting and lying
And be compassionate, ready to forgive,
Just as I have forgiven you. (Eph 4:31–32)

As you were forgiven and rescued from
    the power of sin, (Col 1:13–15)
Condemn to death all the bad things you
    do (Rom 8:13)
For what benefit did you ever gain from
    doing that
Which you are now ashamed of?
    (Rom 6:21)
Consider yourself dead to sin, but alive to
    Me for evermore. (Rom 6:11)
You have died with Christ and are freed
    from the power of sin,
But as you have died, know that you
    shall also live with Him. (Rom 6:7–8)

Your old life, so full of sin, has died –
Your old self was buried with My Son
So, as you were baptized into His death
How can you still live the way you used
    to?
As Christ was raised by Me,
So do you also have new life. (Rom 6:2–6)

You must put away lying, My child.
    (Eph 4:25)
Be wise and do not be quickly provoked
    to anger; (Eccl 7:9)

Do not stay angry with anyone,
    (Eph 4:26)

For this is what you used to be like,

But now you have been washed,
    sanctified and justified

In the name of My Son, by Our Spirit,
    (1 Cor 6:11)

The Spirit of holiness. (Rom 1:4)

Do not lie, for you have removed your old
    self

And put on the new, renewed self, which
    becomes ever richer as it grows

In knowledge of Me who created it.
    (Col 3:9–10)

You cannot carry on sinning as you used
    to,

For you have been born into My family.
    (1 John 3:9)

I have not chosen you to be anything but
    pure –

So lead a holy life, My child. (1 Thess 4:7)

No child of Mine should steal, but work

And share with those who have less.
    (Eph 4:28)

Forgive others, just as I have forgiven
    you, and (Col 3:13)

Do not use your body for sinning with,

But offer yourself as My instrument for
    righteous change. (Rom 6:13)

In your natural self you are so weak,

But as you once gave your body as sin's
    slave,

Offer it now to be a slave to
    righteousness. (Rom 6:19)

The new law of the Spirit has freed you
from sin and death, (Rom 8:2)

So set your desires on things above.
(Col 3:1)

Set yourself apart and be made holy by
My Word and by prayer, (1 Tim 4:5)

For My Word is living and powerful.
(Heb 4:12)

My dear child, you know that you should
no longer sin.

But if you do, know also that you have
an Intercessor,

A Mediator to speak on your behalf – the
Righteous One Himself. (1 John 2:1)

Devote yourself to prayer (Col 4:2)

And make My Son Lord in your heart,
(1 Pet 3:15)

Yearn to know My Son more intimately,

To know the power of His resurrection
(Phil 3:10)

And as you are made holy through the
blood He shed, (Heb 13:12)

Aim for perfection in holiness, just as I
am holy. (Matt 5:48)

Live in Love

And you will live in Me

And I in you. (1 John 4:16)

As you are now free from the power of sin

And have offered yourself to do My work,

The benefits you shall receive lead to
holiness,

Resulting in eternal life. (Rom 6:22)

You are being made holy, and because of
My Son's sacrifice for you,

You shall be made forever perfect.
(Heb 10:14)

However, you are not perfect yet, My
child;

But press ahead and you will surely have
all and be all

That has been destined for you. (Phil 3:12)

All My children, (Eph 1:1)

Each of your brothers and sisters,

Are saints in My Son. (Phil 4:21)

You are becoming more and more like Him

And I am making you all the more
glorious through My Spirit in you;
(2 Cor 3:18)

I will achieve in you all that is pleasing to
Me. (Heb 13:21)

I will sanctify you completely

And keep you without blame before My
returning Son, (1 Thess 5:23)

For life itself works within you.
(2 Cor 4:12)

Obedient to the truth, you have been
purified,

So love all of My children,

Love your brothers and sisters deeply,
from your heart. (1 Pet 1:22)

Submit yourself to My correction and
discipline (Heb 12:9)

For your name is written in heaven

And your spirit, being made righteous, is
becoming flawless. (Heb 12:23)

I have begun this great work within you

And you can be assured that I will
complete it. (Phil 1:6)

Just as everything that Jesus had on this
earth came from Me, (John 17:7)

My grace and peace (Col 1:2)

And fullness in Christ I give to you.
(Col 2:10)

When you are ready, I will teach you
about righteousness. (Heb 5:13–14)

I will make your love for each other
increase to overflowing. (1 Thess 3:12)

I am the God of peace,

I will sanctify you wholly and fully
(1 Thess 5:23)

And when you see Christ again all your
faults will vanish. (1 Cor 13:10)

I will guide you and afterwards

I will bring you to be with Me. (Ps 73:24)

You must suffer a little while longer on
this earth,

But I will complete you, making you
strong and determined. (1 Pet 5:10)

For trials will come, but I will only allow
those that you can bear. (1 Cor 10:13)

My child, simply believe and everything
will be possible. (Mark 9:23)

I am Father to the fatherless,

Defender of the vulnerable (Ps 68:5)

And you should be the same so that I
may work through you. (Phil 2:13)

Entrust your plans to Me and you will
succeed. (Prov 16:3)

Set apart, you will be My most useful
 instrument,
Made holy for good and noble work.
 (2 Tim 2:21)

I will equip you with everything you need
 to do My will. (Heb 13:21)
Fear not, I shall strengthen your heart
 (1 Thess 3:13)
And as My child
You will overcome the world. (1 John 5:4)

Love, your Father,
Almighty God

11 The Church, My Son's Promised Bride

My Dear Child,

You are called to be holy and united with
all My children (1 Cor 1:2)
So take your place among those who are
sanctified
By their faith in My Son, (Acts 26:18)
With all who call on Jesus –
For He is both your Lord and theirs.
(1 Cor 1:2)

You have all been baptized by My Spirit
into one body, My church;
All My children have been given the same
Spirit to drink. (1 Cor 12:13)
I am your God, the Father of your Lord,
Through My loving kindness you were
reborn into a living hope (1 Pet 1:3)
And given the gift of My very own Spirit.
(Acts 2:38)

Let peace rule in your heart, (Col 3:15)
And listen to the words of My Spirit.
(Rev 2:7)

By your new birth, you have entered the
  church, My child
And your name is written in heaven.
  (Heb 12:23)

Do not be the cause of anyone's failures,
No matter what their background.
  (1 Cor 10:32)
For here in the church there is no
  difference between anyone –
My Son is everything and in everyone.
  (Col 3:11)

My Son is building His church
  (Matt 16:18)
And every day I add all those I have saved
To their number. (Acts 2:47)
By Our Spirit you have been baptized into
  the body of Christ. (1 Cor 12:13)
By their belief, My sons and daughters are
  added. (Acts 5:14)

My children are a holy nation,
Chosen to be My Royal priesthood.
  (1 Pet 2:9)
Citizens of heaven, (Phil 3:20)
You are not of this world. (John 17:14)
Christ has set you free from your sins
And is making you into a Kingdom of
  priests,
Ready to serve your Father in heaven.
  (Rev 1:5–6)
You belong to Me so that you may boldly
  praise My Son
Who called you into His glorious light.
  (1 Pet 2:9)

He loves His church as a husband loves
    his wife

And gave Himself up for her to save her
    and make her holy.

He will soon present her to Himself –

A radiant bride, a church without blemish –

Both holy and innocent. (Eph 5:25–27)

When the time comes,

When the bride has made herself ready,

The wedding will commence

And you will have the greatest joy.
    (Rev 19:7)

For the Bridegroom is the very King
    Himself, the Lord of lords, (Rev 19:16)

The very Word of God. (Rev 19:13)

She is His very body

And He is both her Head and Saviour.
    (Eph 5:23)

For her sake I have placed everything
    under His feet. (Eph 1:22)

Truly, everyone invited to this wedding
    celebration is blessed indeed, (Rev 19:9)

For the union of Christ and His bride is a
    profound mystery. (Eph 5:32)

As I present the pure church to her
    promised Husband, (2 Cor 11:2)

She should submit herself to Him,
    (Eph 5:24)

For you cannot be joined to both the ways
    of the world,

To seeking pleasure and success at all
    costs,

And also to Christ: this is adulterous.
  (Jas 4:4)

My Spirit lives in every one of My
  children, (1 Cor 3:16)
And everyone is being built into My
  spiritual house;
You are like living stones. (1 Pet 2:5)

You have been laid upon the foundation of
  My apostles and prophets, (Eph 2:20)
Some of whom were hunted, some beaten
  and some killed. (Matt 23:34)
Christ Himself is the building's most
  important Stone and (Eph 2:20–21)
This Foundation cannot be replaced.
  (1 Cor 3:11)
Through Him the entire building rises in
  unity
As My children are constructed into a
  home
Fit for Our Spirit. (Eph 2:21–22)

Your foundation is on rock, nothing can
  make you fall
For you have heard My Son's words and
  apply them in your life. (Matt 7:24–25)
All My children drink from this same
  spiritual Rock,
For this Rock is My Son. (1 Cor 10:4)

I will enlighten the eyes of your heart so
  you may know
The hope to which you have been called.
  (Eph 1:18)
As you have such a hope – be bold!
  (2 Cor 3:12)

What was once so glorious, is nothing at
   all
Compared with that which surpasses all –
The everlasting glory! (2 Cor 3:10–11)

Just as it has been from the very beginning
My children, the church, devote
   themselves to
My teaching, their fellowship, to prayer
   and to the Lord's Supper. (Acts 2:42)
My Son and My Spirit both urge you to
Pray for the people you know.
   (Rom 15:30)

Participate in the Lord's Supper, the body
   and blood of the Christ. (1 Cor 10:16)
His body is the living bread come from
   heaven,
If you eat of this you will surely live
   forever. (John 6:51)
Examine yourself and then (1 Cor 11:28)
Take and eat – it is His body,
Drink from the blood of the covenant,
   (Matt 26:26–28)
The new covenant in His blood,
   (Luke 22:20)
Divide it among you (Luke 22:17)
Remembering what My Son has
   accomplished for you; (Luke 22:19)
For He has bought Our church with His
   blood. (Acts 20:28)

Fill your mind with thoughts of whatever
   is pure,
Whatever is noble and true,

Whatever is excellent or worthy of praise,
(Phil 4:8)

And help prepare My children for their
service

So that Christ's body is fully developed,
instructed and enlightened

Growing in faith and the knowledge of
My Son, (Eph 4:12–13)

Speaking the truth in love, (Eph 4:15)

Becoming mature and desiring to achieve
all it can be, (Eph 4:13)

Overflowing with gratitude and
thankfulness. (Col 2:7)

I give gifts to everyone in the church:

Some can teach, some can heal and some
can help. (1 Cor 12:28)

But whatever you do,

Work alongside Me (1 Cor 3:9)

Without complaint or argument

So that you are without fault in this
world. (Phil 2:14–15)

Be strong and brave,

Do not be discouraged,

Paralysed by your fear. (1 Chr 22:13)

But be My witness of the suffering, dying
and risen Christ,

And to the fact of sin's forgiveness to all
who turn to Me. (Luke 24:46–48)

All that people must do is confess, 'Jesus
is Lord',

And believe that I raised Him from the
dead,

And they will be saved. (Rom 10:9)

They will receive the Spirit just as you
    have, (Acts 10:47)

And they too will be My very own
    children

Through their faith in My Son. (Gal 3:26)

Have you not been told to deliver this
    good news? (Rom 10:15)

You have been sent – go and make
    disciples from every country.
    (Matt 28:19)

Go into all creation and tell everyone My
    good news, (Mark 16:15)

My witnesses must go out to the very
    ends of the earth, (Acts 1:8)

And baptize into My family all who
    believe, both man and woman,
    (Acts 8:12)

In the name of your Father, My Son and
    the Holy Spirit. (Matt 28:19)

Entrust what I have told you to reliable
    people;

They will then be qualified to teach still
    more. (2 Tim 2:2)

Just as My Son is the great Shepherd
    (Heb 13:20)

So shall you also guard My children.
    (Acts 20:28)

Be, yourself, a shepherd to My flock.
    (1 Pet 5:2)

Love, your Father,
Almighty God

12 My Son Shall Return Soon

My Dear Child,

When the time comes for Me to restore
  and perfect everything
I will send My Son once more,
Just as I promised many years ago.
  (Acts 3:21)
Tell everyone to turn to Me so their sins
  may be no more and
I can send the Christ. (Acts 3:19–20)
Tell the whole world My good news,
And then the end will come. (Matt 24:14)

My Son will return with My own great
  glory (Matt 16:27)
And take you home,
So that you may be where We are.
  (John 14:3)
Listen to this mystery:
Not all of My children will fall asleep
But all will be transformed (1 Cor 15:51)
And gathered to My Son. (2 Thess 2:1)
Know that all My children who are alive
  at the time

Will be caught up together in the clouds
And meet My Son, your Lord, in the air.
   (1 Thess 4:17)

Comfort and encourage one another with
   these words (1 Thess 4:18)
For in a very short time,
My Son will come to you. (Heb 10:37)
Your complete salvation is close at hand,
Nearer now than when you first accepted
   Me. (Rom 13:11)

My child, in these times you hear of so
   many wars and rumours of wars,
Earthquakes and famines, natural
   disasters and tragedies
But do not worry, terrible as these things
   are, this must happen,
For in these end-times, nation will rise
   against nation. (Matt 24:6–7)
But always be on watch,
Praying that you may escape all that is to
   occur. (Luke 21:36)

Not everyone will believe,
Many will ask when this 'promised
   coming' will happen,
Because, to them, everything appears to
   carry on as normal,
Just as it always has. (2 Pet 3:4)
But learn from this:
When you see leaves forming on the
   tender branches of trees
You know that summer is close at hand;
Similarly, when you see these things that
   I have told you about, (Matt
   24:32–33)

When the time of unequalled distress
     occurs, (Matt 24:21)
Know that the time is near,
My Son is right at the door. (Matt 24:33)

Keep watch My child, (Mark 13:37)
Stay alert and self-controlled, calm and
     collected (1 Thess 5:6)
So that you may stand confidently and
     unashamedly before Him.
     (1 John 2:28)
For He will come suddenly and
     unannounced,
Perhaps at dawn, maybe at midnight.
     (Mark 13:35–36)
He will return on the day you least expect,
At an hour you do not know; (Matt 24:50)
For it is Me who chooses the appointed
     time, (Ps 75:2)
Nobody knows the exact time but Me.
     (Matt 24:36)
Be patient and resolute, for the time is
     near. (Jas 5:8)
When He appears you shall see Him as He
     truly is
And you too will be like Him. (1 John 3:2)

Wait eagerly by faith through the Spirit.
     (Gal 5:5)
For this is your blessed hope – (Titus 2:13)
And as you have this hope in you,
You purify yourself. (1 John 3:3)

My child, set your mind on heavenly
     things,

Remember that you have already died and
    your life is hidden
With My Son in Me;
He is your life and when He appears
You too will appear with Him in glory.
    (Col 3:2–4)

Be careful, My child,
Do not allow your heart to be weighed
    down
With the cares and anxieties of life.
    (Luke 21:34)
He is coming soon,
Guard what you have so that no one can
    take it from you. (Rev 3:11)
Be prepared, (Matt 24:44)
Or this day will come upon you
    unexpectedly. (Luke 21:34)

Do not be ashamed of Him and Our words,
Particularly in this degrading world you
    now live in,
Or He too will be ashamed of you when
    He appears with all My glory.
    (Mark 8:38)
If you endure, you will also reign with
    Him;
If you turn your back on Him, He will
    also disown you. (2 Tim 2:12)
Do not be mistaken, you will have trouble
    in this world,
But be encouraged and accept My peace,
For I am victorious. (John 16:33)

My Son appeared once to eradicate the
    sins of My children (Heb 9:28)

In order for you to be truly holy.
    (John 17:19)
He shall return to bring complete salvation
For all that are His. (Heb 9:28)

My child, as you know that My Son died
    and rose again,
Know also that, when He returns,
I will bring with Christ all My children
    who have fallen asleep. (1 Thess 4:14)
This is not for you to speculate over, for I
    have revealed it:
Be assured that what I have planned will
    surely occur,
Just as I have foreseen. (Isa 14:24)

Wait in eager anticipation, My child,
    (Gal 5:5)
And may you join with all My children in
    saying,
Amen, may it be so. Come, Lord Jesus.
    (Rev 22:20)

Love, your Father,
Almighty God

13 You have Everything to Look Forward To

My Dear Child,

Be confident in this life, (2 Cor 5:8)
With Me, your work will be fruitful
But know also that to depart this life is to
    be with Christ,
And that is much better. (Phil 1:22–23)
Distanced from your body
You will be at home with My Son.
    (2 Cor 5:8)

I do not wish you to have no knowledge
    about death, (1 Thess 4:13)
Physical bodies give birth to physical
    bodies, (John 3:6)
That which returns to the ground.
    (Ps 146:4)
But My Spirit gives birth to spirit,
    (John 3:6)
And that returns to Me. (Eccl 12:7)

Be assured that if your earthly body is
    destroyed
An eternal dwelling waits for you in
    heaven. (2 Cor 5:1)

It is your heavenly body that you desire
  so greatly,

For when you are clothed in this,

You shall never ache again with your
  burden.

When you are home, you shall not be
  found wanting, (2 Cor 5:2–4)

My Son will receive your spirit. (Acts 7:59)

When My Son comes to earth,

Riding on the clouds of heaven, (Dan 7:13)

With a loud shout

He will command all those who have fallen
  asleep in Him to rise. (1 Thess 4:16)

By My power, I raised My Son

And I will raise you also. (1 Cor 6:14)

I have not told you everything

But you know that when He appears you
  will be just as He is. (1 John 3:2)

You and all creation will see the glory of
  God,

The great Jesus Christ; (Titus 2:13)

Everyone will see Him, (Rev 1:7)

Even those in their graves will hear His
  voice, (John 5:28)

Even the very ones who crucified Him.
  (Rev 1:7)

Just as lightning is visible both in the east
  and the west, (Matt 24:27)

So will the sign of My Son be seen in the
  sky. (Matt 24:30)

The dead will be raised indestructible,
  permanent,

And all My children will be changed in a
moment. (1 Cor 15:51–52)

Your earthly bodies will be transformed,
(Phil 3:21)

For He is the resurrection and the life.
(John 11:25)

So let your faith and hope be in Me
(1 Pet 1:21)

And honour Him just as you honour Me.
(John 5:22–23)

You have the first fruits, the first benefits,
of Our Spirit My child,

Now you must eagerly wait for the
redemption of your body,

For in this hope you are saved.
(Rom 8:23–24)

But how will the dead be raised

And what will their bodies be like?
(1 Cor 15:35)

You will have flesh and bones, My child,
(Luke 24:39)

But gloriously transformed like the body
of My Son. (Phil 3:21)

My faithful children will be resurrected
and with Christ for a thousand years,

Then everyone else in their grave will be
raised –

Happy and holy, truly to be envied,

Are My children who take part in this
first resurrection. (Rev 20:4–6)

The vast multitudes asleep in the grave
will awake (Dan 12:2)

And death itself, the final enemy,
(1 Cor 15:26)

Will be swallowed up by My Son's
victory, (Isa 25:8)

Mortality being clothed with immortality.
(1 Cor 15:53)

You must tell everyone: (Acts 10:42)

As He is the true Son of Man, (John 5:27)

I have appointed Him to be Judge of both
the living and the dead, (Acts 10:42)

I have appointed My Son to judge the
world with perfect justice;

Your proof is that I have raised Him from
the grave. (Acts 17:31)

Be glad and let Me hear you sing,

For I come to judge the earth with
fairness. (Ps 98:9)

Everyone from around the world will be
brought before My Son, (Matt 25:32)

All must take their place before the
judgement seat. (2 Cor 5:10)

But have peace, My child, because your
punishment was borne by Him.
(Isa 53:5)

I have put all the sins He bore behind My
back, (Isa 38:17)

They have all gone, (Acts 3:19)

I have stamped on them and thrown
them out to sea. (Mic 7:19)

My Son, the great Shepherd, will separate
the people before Him:

His sheep will be led to their inheritance

For they followed Christ and were blessed
by Me,

But the goats will be sent to their eternal
punishment. (Matt 25:32–34, 41, 46)

All who return to the dust will kneel
    before Him, (Ps 22:29)
All will stand before My throne with the
    books of their lives before Me.
Death will give up the dead,
And all will be judged according to their
    endeavours. (Rev 20:12–13)
I will judge every nation, (Ps 110:6)
Every secret deed, through My Son.
    (Rom 2:16)

But there will be another book present on
    that day –
The book of life. (Rev 20:12)
My child, you believe in Me who raised
    My Son from the dead;
For this you shall be reckoned righteous
    (Rom 4:24)
And included in its pages. (Rev 3:5)

Those who do not know Me,
Those who do not obey My Son,
Will be punished. (2 Thess 1:7–8)
But to all who persist in doing good
He will give eternal life. (Rom 2:7)

On that day, your life's work will be
    shown for what it is
And, if what you have built survives, you
    will receive your reward.
    (1 Cor 3:13–14)
I will reward each of My children,
According to what they have done.
    (Rom 2:6)

As you have been raised with Christ, My
  child,

Seek and pursue the treasures from
  above, where My Son is with Me.
  (Col 3:1)

Persevere! For when you have fulfilled My
  will

You will receive My promise. (Heb 10:36)

Place your hope in the unimaginable
  riches of your inheritance,

And in My own great power.
  (Eph 1:18–19)

My Son is the Heir of all things, and
  (Heb 1:2)

You will be richly welcomed into Our
  Kingdom. (2 Pet 1:11)

For, as you are My child,

So are you also My heir. (Rom 8:17)

You are born into an imperishable
  inheritance,

Which, through your faith, is guarded by
  Me

Until the time is right to reveal it.
  (1 Pet 1:4–5)

To all who yearn for His appearing,
  (2 Tim 4:8)

To all who are forever faithful, (Jas 1:12)

I have in store a crown of righteousness,
  (2 Tim 4:8)

A crown of life, (Jas 1:12)

An everlasting crown of glory. (1 Pet 5:4)

My Son is preparing a home for you in
  My great house, (John 14:2)

You will forever share in My Son's
  happiness. (Matt 25:21)

Love, your Father,
Almighty God

14 The End and the New Beginning

My Dear Child,

This universe you know will be destroyed
   by fire;
With a terrible sound,
Its elements will be burnt up in the heat
   (2 Pet 3:10)
And I will make all things anew. (Rev 21:5)
My Son will subject Himself to Me
And I will be everything and in everything.
   (1 Cor 15:28)

Do not hide these words of Mine from
   your children, (Ps 78:4)
But allow Me to make My appeal through
   you
And implore the world to make peace
   with their Father. (2 Cor 5:20)
Clothe yourself with compassion and
   kindness,
Gentleness, humility and patience.
   (Col 3:12)
And to this, add Our peace and grace.
   (Rom 1:7)

Study My Word to see if what has been
said is true, (Acts 17:11)

Test everything – discard what is false
(1 Thess 5:21)

And be prepared to explain the hope you
have to everyone who asks,

But do so with tenderness and respect.
(1 Pet 3:15)

The new heavens and earth will be so
wonderful, My child,

No one will prefer the old, they will be
forgotten. (Isa 65:17)

But the new universe will remain forever,

Together with all My children. (Isa 66:22)

The new heavens and earth will be the
very home of righteousness.
(2 Pet 3:13)

The holy city will descend from My
hands, down from heaven.

I will live with My children and they will
live with Me.

No more shall there be any sorrow or pain,

For the old world,

The way things are now, will be destroyed

And all things will be made new.
(Rev 21:2–5)

Like Abraham,

Look forward to this divine city, designed
and built by Me. (Heb 11:10)

The river of life, as bright as crystal, will
flow from Our throne, (Rev 22:1)

Feeding the tree of life and its efficacious
leaves. (Rev 22:2)

All who desire may drink from the river
(Rev 22:17)

And eat from the tree of life. (Rev 22:19)

You will shine like the sun, My child.
(Matt 13:43)

There will be no need for a sun or a moon

For My glory shall be your light and My
Son your lamp. (Rev 21:23)

All nations will see by My light,
(Rev 21:24)

And you shall reign forever. (Rev 22:5)

When the bride is made ready and clothed
in radiant white, (Rev 19:7–8)

In a gown interwoven with gold,
(Ps 45:13)

Bright with the righteous work of My
saints, (Rev 19:8)

With all who persevere to victory, (Rev 3:5)

The wedding ceremony will commence.
(Rev 19:7)

For the bride, the future wife of My Son,
(Rev 21:9)

Belongs to the Bridegroom (John 3:29)

And the two shall become one.
(Eph 5:31–32)

As the waters cover the sea, so will the
knowledge of Me fill the earth,

And nothing will ever harm or destroy
again. (Isa 11:9)

When all things are made new

You shall join My Son on glorious
thrones. (Matt 19:28)

My dear child, I gave My own Son for you,

Will I not also give you everything else?
   (Rom 8:32)

With all My love, your Father,
Almighty God

Acknowledgements

The concept of this book owes its inspiration to the *Father's Love Letter*, a short and beautiful letter written by Barry Adams expressing the 'cry of a Father's heart' to His children.

I delved deeply into many English translations of the Bible, textbooks of theology, Bible concordances and other sources to research and understand the key Bible verses needed to compose these *Letters*. Among these sources were the *Systematic Theology* textbooks of Thiessen, Berkhof, Strong and Hodge and the following versions of the Bible: *New International Version, Today's New International Version, King James Version, New King James Version, 21st Century King James Version, New Living Translation, Amplified Bible, The Message, New Life Version, Contemporary English Version, English Standard Version, New American Standard Bible, Holman Christian Standard Bible, Young's Literal Translation, Darby Translation* and *Wycliffe New Testament*.

My deepest gratitude goes to the authors, translators and publishers of all these works. I also thank Alex Sanderson for his dedication in taking the time to thoroughly review each of the verses, my paraphrases and their doctrinal implications in the early drafts of this book.

Appendix 1

A description of the topics covered in these *Letters from Home*

The scripture index that follows gives the number of the *Letter* in which the particular verses can be found. Each *Letter* is concerned with a different topic of the Christian faith and these topics will be known to academic students as the traditional divisions of systematic theology. These divisions and topics of the *Letters* are shown here, below their titles.

1 **A Little About Me**

   Concerning the Nature of God

2 **I Created You and All You See**

   Concerning the Works of God 1 – Creation

3 **I am in Control**

   Concerning the Works of God 2 – Preservation

4 **Your Disobedient Condition**

   Concerning Sin and the Nature of Man

5 **We have been Reconciled, Turn to Me**

   Concerning Soteriology, the Plan of Salvation

Appendix 2

Index of Scripture References

Psalms

2:10	3	103:14	2
3:5	3	103:17	1; 3
4:8	3	104:6	2
9:8	3	104:21	3
16:10	7	104:24	2
17:15	1	104:27	3
19:1–3	2	104:30	2
19:7	3; 4	110:6	13
22:9–10	7	111:2	2
22:24	7	111:4	1
22:28	3	115:3	1
22:29	13	119:18	5
33:6	2	119:64	2
33:13–15	1	119:137	3
33:14–15	3	119:142	3
36:6	3	119:160	3
36:9	2	127:2	3
37:28	5	139:3–7	1
40:11	2	139:7–10	8
45:13	14	139:13	2
46:11	1	139:15–16	2
51:6	8	139:16	9
55:22	1	139:17–18	1
58:3	4	145:16	1
66:7	3	145:18	1
68:5	10	146:4	13
71:6	2	147:9	3
73:24	10	147:18	3
75:2	12		
75:7	3	**Proverbs**	
78:4	14	3:5–6	1
78:29	4	3:19	2
89:14	1	5:21	1
90:2	1	5:22	4
90:4	1	15:3	1
93:2	1	16:3	10
98:9	13	21:2	4
100:3	2		
102:25	2	**Ecclesiastes**	
102:26–27	3	12:7	13
102:27	1		

13:21	**10**	3:10	**14**
		3:13	**14**
James			
1:12	**13**	**1 John**	
1:13	**1**	1:5	**1**
1:16–17	**3**	1:7	**5**
4:4	**11**	1:8	**4**
4:8	**5**	1:9	**5**
4:10	**5**	2:1	**10**
5:8	**12**	2:6	**6; 9**
		2:13	**6**
1 Peter		2:20	**8**
1:3	**11**	2:23	**5**
1:4–5	**13**	2:27	**8**
1:6	**2**	2:28	**12**
1:20	**7**	3:1	**9**
1:21	**13**	3:2	**12; 13**
1:22	**10**	3:3	**12**
2:5	**11**	3:4–5	**5**
2:9	**11**	3:5	**6**
2:21	**6**	3:9	**10**
2:22	**7**	3:23	**9**
2:23	**7**	4:2	**8**
2:24	**5; 7**	4:10	**6; 7**
2:25	**9**	4:13	**9**
3:15	**10; 14**	4:16	**9; 10**
3:18	**5**	5:4	**10**
3:22	**7**	5:12	**5**
4:10	**8**		
4:11	**6**	**2 John**	
5:2	**11**	1:7	**6**
5:7	**1; 3**		
5:10	**10**	**Revelation**	
5:14	**13**	1:5–6	**11**
		1:7	**7; 13**
2 Peter		1:8	**6**
1:4	**9**	1:17	**6**
1:11	**13**	2:7	**11**
2:9	**2**	2:8	**7**
3:4	**12**	3:5	**13; 14**
3:8	**1**	3:11	**12**
3:9	**3**	4:11	**2**